CANCEL CULTURE

SOCIAL JUSTICE or MOB RULE?

John Allen

ReferencePoint
Press™

San Diego, CA

About the Author

John Allen is a writer who lives in Oklahoma City.

For more information, contact:
ReferencePoint Press, Inc.
PO Box 27779
San Diego, CA 92198
www.ReferencePointPress.com

LIBRARY OF CONGRESS CATALOGING-IN-PUBLICATION DATA

Names: Allen, John, 1957- author.
Title: Cancel culture : social justice or mob rule? / John Allen.
Description: San Diego, CA : ReferencePoint Press, Inc., 2022. | Includes
    bibliographical references and index.
Identifiers: LCCN 2021037195 (print) | LCCN 2021037196 (ebook) | ISBN
    9781678202347 (library binding) | ISBN 9781678202354 (ebook)
Subjects: LCSH: Cancel culture--Juvenile literature. | Social
    media--Political aspects--Juvenile literature.
Classification: LCC HM1176 .A45 2022 (print) | LCC HM1176 (ebook) | DDC
    302/.13--dc23
LC record available at https://lccn.loc.gov/2021037195
LC ebook record available at https://lccn.loc.gov/2021037196

CONTENTS

Introduction   4
A Controversial Trend

Chapter One   8
What Is Cancel Culture?

Chapter Two   20
The #MeToo Movement

Chapter Three   32
Cancel Culture and Political Speech

Chapter Four   43
Reexamining the Past

Source Notes   55
Differing Views: Accountability or Punishment?   58
For Further Research   59
Index   61
Picture Credits   64

A Controversial Trend

In February 2021 Georgetown University law professor Sandra Sellers addressed a sensitive issue in a private talk on Zoom. Sellers was worried about the performance of certain Black students in her classes. Although some were doing well, others were falling behind, and she found this discouraging. "I hate to say this," she told her colleague, "I end up having this angst every semester that a lot of my lower ones are blacks—happens almost every semester."[1] Sellers was referring to lower grades. Her discussion touched on how the law school might better prepare minority students for success.

Sellers did not realize that her Zoom exchange was being recorded. A video clip of her remarks about Black students' low grades was posted to Twitter by Hassan Ahmad, a law student at Georgetown. Ahmad added a caption: "@GeorgetownLaw negotiations professors Sandra Sellers and David Batson being openly racist on a recorded Zoom call. Beyond unacceptable."[2]

Twitter outrage erupted at once. Georgetown's Black Law Students Association gathered one thousand signatures on a petition demanding that Sellers be fired. William Treanor, head of Georgetown's law school, condemned Sellers's comments. The day after the post appeared, Treanor fired Sellers with no further investigation. Media outlets debated the case along predictable lines. Some saw the incident as a victory for social justice. Others regarded it as so-called cancel culture gone out of control.

A Push for Accountability

Cancel culture refers to the act of punishing individuals, usually by way of social media, for words or actions deemed unacceptable. Whatever its impact, cancel culture owes its rise to social media. Sellers's remarks, which she intended to remain private, reached a huge audience due to the shared video clip on Twitter. Mounting anger over Sellers's alleged racism led to her dismissal. An incident that might once have quickly faded away instead mushroomed into a national story. Sellers herself apologized for what she said were ill-chosen words, and she insisted that she would have resigned had she not been fired. At any rate, her twenty-year teaching career at Georgetown came to a sudden end.

Unlike Sellers, most people targeted by so-called cancel culture are well-known public figures or celebrities. Often, it involves a kind of boycott. When performers are "canceled," online users urge others not to watch their films, buy their music, or attend their concerts. Cancellation can also have more direct results. In some cases, it can lead to a person being fired, banned from social media, or dropped as a company spokesperson. Some suggest that celebrities who are canceled often are able to resume their careers with no real penalty. But the backlash can hit a performer in the pocketbook. In 2018, after her blatantly racist tweet sparked outrage, actress Roseanne Barr was fired from her popular sitcom, at a loss of more than $20 million for the season.

Cancel culture is often linked to a "woke" political outlook. This refers to having progressive beliefs and advocating for social justice in society. In fact, some reject the term *cancel culture* in favor of *call-out culture*—or calling out those who express hateful views, post racist jokes or material, or insist on demeaning certain groups. They see social media protests as a way for those who once lacked a voice in society to hold people accountable for their behavior. The #MeToo movement targeted celebrities who were accused of sexual assault or harassment. As more victims of

"It reinforces, at a time of political division, a sense of shared solidarity, at least among the people who are doing the canceling."[3]

—Jill McCorkel, professor of sociology and criminology at Villanova University

sexual misconduct shared their stories, public opinion swelled to support them. Among those called out by #MeToo accusers were Hollywood producer Harvey Weinstein, actor Kevin Spacey, conservative political host Bill O'Reilly, and filmmaker Woody Allen. Weinstein was convicted of sexual assault and went to prison.

Joining together with like-minded individuals to point out unacceptable speech or behavior can also bring feelings of shared purpose. "It reinforces, at a time of political division, a sense of shared solidarity, at least among the people who are doing the canceling," says Jill McCorkel, a professor of sociology and criminology at Vil-

Cancel culture, viewed by some as social justice and others as mob rule, refers to the act of punishing individuals for words or actions deemed unacceptable. It owes its rise to social media.

lanova University. "It's psychologically intoxicating to feel part of a group and to feel a part of something larger than yourself."[3]

Concerns About Free Speech

Critics of cancel culture question whether woke solidarity too often becomes a sort of mob justice online. A clumsy tweet, a show of support for a disfavored person, even an off-color joke dredged up from a decade ago can result in an avalanche of condemnation. Conservatives often claim to be the main targets of the woke tide. They insist that cancel culture tends to chill open debate by attacking views considered to be politically incorrect.

Free speech advocates also worry that people are becoming reluctant to share strong opinions in public for fear of a backlash and possible loss of a job or career. Such fears are found across the political spectrum. In July 2020 more than 150 artists, writers, journalists, and intellectuals signed "A Letter on Justice and Open Debate" in *Harper's Magazine*. The letter warned about a growing climate of intolerance for opposing views. Some applauded this plea for free speech values. But others noted that the high-profile figures who signed the letter certainly have no problem expressing their views for a large audience.

The debate about cancel culture has even reached high school and middle school students. A report in the *New York Times* revealed that many teens have mixed feelings about the trend.

"Being 'called in' instead of 'called out' is a much more effective way to help members of our society grow and become better people in the future."[4]

—A teen writer in a *New York Times* forum on cancel culture

Several expressed a wish for more forgiveness. "Problematic actions need to be addressed in a way that gently leads people to understand their errors instead of aggressively calling people out publicly," wrote one teen. "Being 'called in' instead of 'called out' is a much more effective way to help members of our society grow and become better people in the future."[4]

CHAPTER ONE

What Is Cancel Culture?

Comedian Kevin Hart makes his living by delivering edgy comments. He knows that a joke, by definition, has to surprise the audience—maybe even startle it. But in today's politically sensitive climate, edgy humor can be judged as having crossed a line and become offensive. In 2018 Hart experienced a sharp backlash on Twitter and other social media over tweets he had posted nearly a decade before. The tweets included derogatory names for gay people and off-color remarks about gay sexuality. The social media storm and resulting publicity caused Hart to step down as host of that year's Academy Awards ceremony. However, Hart's brush with cancel culture did not permanently damage his career. He continued to appear in podcasts, commercials, and movies, and he plans to resume touring with his comedy routine. "I've been canceled, what, three or four times?" says Hart. "Never bothered. If you allow it to have an effect on you, it will. Personally? That's not how I operate. I understand people are human."[5]

Different Meanings for Different People

Although Hart downplays the effects of cancel culture, the concept continues to draw controversy. The term *cancel culture* means different things to different people. Some on the political left dismiss it as a loaded "scare" term that conservatives use to rally their supporters. They note that former president Donald Trump attacked cancel culture in campaign speeches at Mount Rushmore and at the Republican National Convention. Others view the trend as a harmless exchange of opinions online. Political activists relate it to social justice, with Twitter users joining together to call out bad behavior or hate speech. Critics, however, many of them on the political right, view cancel culture as a toxic trend that threatens free speech. They claim its judgmental attacks, whether on celebrities or private citizens, can amount to bullying and harassment.

"I've been canceled, what, three or four times? Never bothered. If you allow it to have an effect on you, it will. Personally? That's not how I operate. I understand people are human."[5]

—Kevin Hart, comedian and film star

Polls show that Americans are deeply divided about cancel culture—that is, if they know about it at all. A February 2021 poll conducted by the Huffington Post and YouGov revealed that nearly half of Americans are not familiar with the term. Among those who know about it, two-thirds believe it is a serious problem. Concern about cancel culture also diverges along political lines. Only 11 percent of Democrats consider it a very serious problem, compared to 57 percent of Republicans and 44 percent of Independents. Forty-four percent of all those polled believe conservatives are more likely than liberals to receive negative effects from cancel culture. More than two-thirds of Republicans agree that conservatives are its main targets.

Despite the recent clamor over cancel culture, many historians and social scientists see it merely as a new form of social boycott. They point out that America has a long tradition of punishing groups or individuals for bad behavior, often by making public accusations and withdrawing financial support. According to Lawrence Glickman, professor of American studies in the Department of History at Cornell University, "This is one of the oldest forms of political activism in the United States, using the power of the purse to transform the political landscape."[6]

Borrowing from Black Culture

According to some sources, the notion of canceling someone for unacceptable behavior has roots in Black culture. As far back as 1981, Nile Rodgers, guitarist for the funk band Chic, recorded the single "Your Love Is Cancelled," describing how he was dropping a love interest from his life. In the 1991 film *New Jack City*, Wesley Snipes's gangster character announces he is canceling his girlfriend, or dumping her. From there, the term worked its way into a 2010 hip-hop song by Lil Wayne and a 2014 episode of the reality show *Love and Hip-Hop: New York*. These joking references soon turned up on Twitter, as users declared their friends to be canceled for a dumb remark or bad taste. Fi-

> "This is one of the oldest forms of political activism in the United States, using the power of the purse to transform the political landscape."[6]
>
> —Lawrence Glickman, professor of American studies at Cornell University

nally, it spread to more serious usage. Celebrities or politicians who were judged to have made bigoted or insensitive comments got canceled, as did those accused of exploiting minorities or women. Black activists embraced canceling as a kind of empowerment, a way to publicly reject politicians or performers who had lost support in the Black community. Typical was a 2016 tweet about rapper Kanye West, who had expressed support for Trump's candidacy: "I was blasting *Fade* by Kanye and then I remembered he's cancelled and changed."[7] Soon other groups adopted the political edge of cancel culture to express their own disapproval of certain figures.

How People Define Cancel Culture

In May 2021 the Pew Research Center published results of a poll on public attitudes toward cancel culture. The 44 percent of US adults who said they had heard a fair amount or a great deal about cancel culture, were asked to provide their own definition of that term. The largest percentage of respondents, 49 percent, described cancel culture as "actions taken to hold others accountable."

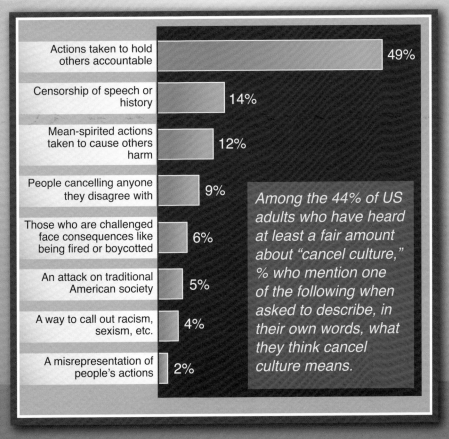

Actions taken to hold others accountable	49%
Censorship of speech or history	14%
Mean-spirited actions taken to cause others harm	12%
People cancelling anyone they disagree with	9%
Those who are challenged face consequences like being fired or boycotted	6%
An attack on traditional American society	5%
A way to call out racism, sexism, etc.	4%
A misrepresentation of people's actions	2%

Among the 44% of US adults who have heard at least a fair amount about "cancel culture," % who mention one of the following when asked to describe, in their own words, what they think cancel culture means.

Source: Emily A. Vogels et al., "Americans and 'Cancel Culture': Where Some See Calls for Accountability, Others See Censorship, Punishment," Pew Research Center, May 19, 2021. www.pewresearch.org.

Social media has been key to the rise of cancel culture. The immediacy of Twitter, Instagram, Facebook, and other platforms enables users to jump into the cultural conversation in real time. Twitter in particular has become a weather vane for attitudes about people in the news. No sooner does a controversial remark or action come

Musician Kanye West (pictured in 2016 with president-elect Donald Trump) had publicly voiced support for Trump's campaign. Fans who were unhappy with this stance considered West to be canceled and stopped listening to his music.

to light than the so-called Twitterverse reacts in cascading numbers. On Twitter, success for calling out someone for bad behavior is measured in likes and retweets, which can quickly mount into the thousands. By contrast, a comment that takes issue with a swarm of cancellation calls can get ratioed. That means getting more replies than likes. It usually indicates that many users reject the comment and feel the need to explain why. Often the commenter is accused of being divisive or misguided.

Certain Black artists and intellectuals connect cancel culture to wider concerns about civil rights and having a voice in society. Screenwriter Barry Michael Cooper, who wrote Wesley Snipes's famous line about cancellation in *New Jack City*, is amazed at how the whole idea of canceling someone has spread. He sees it as an example of Black humor and pride. Announcing that someone is canceled is like changing the channel, refusing to listen to the same old messages. For African Americans, cancellation is "a way to wield power, where we haven't been able to really do it before on a cultural level," says Cooper. "Twitter has allowed us to say, 'We're here, we're not going to be discounted, and if you say anything to try to diminish us, we'll cancel you.'"[8]

Many have noted that the term *woke*, as shorthand for a progressive political outlook, also comes from Black culture. It originally referred to seeing the truth behind the official story, the things that those in power do not want people to know. In 2014, protests about the police shooting of Michael Brown in Ferguson, Missouri, urged Blacks to "stay woke," or be aware of alleged police brutality. The phrase goes back to a 1938 song by the Black folksinger Lead Belly, describing a lynching in the South and warning Blacks to beware. Modern singers such as Erykah Badu and Childish Gambino have urged listeners to "stay woke" in their songs. In the past few years, *woke* has come to mean an emphasis on social justice. As Twitter and other social media platforms have embraced cancel culture, the influence of left-leaning woke political ideas has grown.

> "Twitter has allowed [African Americans] to say, 'We're here, we're not going to be discounted, and if you say anything to try to diminish us, we'll cancel you.'"[8]
>
> —Barry Michael Cooper, screenwriter

Cancellation and Consequences

Canceling may have begun as an offhand way to reject people for insensitive remarks or bad behavior. However, as the trend has taken root, cancellation has occasionally delivered real consequences. The most obvious examples come from the #MeToo movement, in which victims came forward to accuse high-profile individuals of sexual assault and harassment. Many of those accused lost their jobs, and a few have gone to jail. But other targets of cancel culture have also felt the effects of public censure.

A Conservative Cancellation

Conservatives often paint cancel culture as a purely woke phenomenon, but people can get canceled by conservative backlash as well. One example is the case of Colin Kaepernick, a National Football League (NFL) quarterback who led the San Francisco 49ers to the Super Bowl in 2012. Four years later, Kaepernick, then a backup for the 49ers, sparked right-wing anger over his protests against police violence against Blacks. Kaepernick and a few teammates chose to express their views by kneeling during the national anthem. Conservative pundits lashed out at what they characterized as an unpatriotic display. As player protests during the anthem grew, there was talk on the political right of boycotting NFL games. Eric Reid, Kaepernick's teammate at the time, claimed that the protests were being twisted into something they were not. "Our protest is still being misconstrued as disrespectful to the country, flag and military personnel," said Reid. "It's exactly the opposite."

In 2017 Kaepernick opted out of his 49ers contract. None of the other thirty-one NFL teams signed him, effectively ending his football career. Some observers questioned whether the team owners had colluded to oust a troublemaker from the league. As for Kaepernick, he is now a well-paid spokesperson for the sporting goods giant Nike.

Eric Reid, "Eric Reid: Why Colin Kaepernick and I Decided to Take a Knee," *New York Times*, September 25, 2017. www.nytimes.com.

In May 2020 a squabble in New York's Central Park led to a woman losing her job. An African American man named Christian Cooper was enjoying the evening as an expert birdwatcher when he asked Amy Cooper (no relation) to put her dog on a leash, as park rules require. The woman, who is White, refused. In fact, she grew increasingly hysterical as the man insisted that her dog be leashed. Finally, Amy Cooper called the police to say that an African American man was threatening her life. A video, filmed by Christian Cooper and posted to Twitter, was viewed more than 30 million times in the days that followed. Many people saw the incident as an example of how Blacks are falsely accused and placed in danger themselves. The woman was widely mocked as a "Karen"—slang for an entitled middle-aged White woman making demands. As the video went viral, the Twitter backlash led to the woman getting fired from her job despite making a public apology. As for Christian Cooper, he expressed sympathy for her and felt the storm of criticism had gone too far. However, he did say, "I am pretty adamant about not being a participant in my own dehumanization."[9]

At the *New York Times*, woke sensitivities among staff members brought about the firing of a longtime science editor at the paper. The controversy stemmed from a *New York Times*–sponsored student trip to Peru back in 2019. One of the leaders of the trip was Donald McNeil Jr., whose coverage of the coronavirus pandemic was currently drawing widespread praise. In February 2021 reports circulated among the *New York Times* staff that McNeil had repeated aloud a racial slur that one of the students had spoken in relating a story about a friend's offensive language. The students, all of whom were White, apparently were shocked that McNeil had said the word.

Staff members at the *New York Times* were deeply divided over the incident—mostly between young employees urging that McNeil be fired and older staff who thought the reaction was overblown. In a spirit of zero tolerance for racially charged language, Executive Editor Dean Baquet terminated McNeil, ending a career that had spanned forty-five years. Some observers blamed the *New York Times*'s management. Bill Grueskin, a professor at the Columbia School of Journalism and former editor of the *Wall Street Journal*, tweeted, "It's hard to imagine how the NYT could have done a more complete and efficient job of botching this situation with Donald McNeil and the racial slurs."[10]

In the wake of George Floyd's death at the hands of Minneapolis police and the ensuing Black Lives Matter protests across the nation, the entertainment industry moved quickly to show it would not tolerate racist tweets or posts. In 2020 a number of minor performers were fired or edited out of shows for this reason. In addition, Twitter followers unearthed past transgressions by some A-list celebrities. For example, talk show host Jimmy Fallon came under fire for having appeared in blackface in a *Saturday Night Live* skit two decades before. Fallon apologized, and

As thousands marched in protest of George Floyd's murder by a Minneapolis police officer the entertainment industry began firing or editing out performers who had recently posted racist comments. Past transgressions were also punished.

the furor was soon forgotten. In 2019 Governor Ralph Northam of Virginia had become embroiled in a similar controversy. A photo of two men, one in blackface and one in Ku Klux Klan robes, had appeared in Northam's medical school yearbook. Although it was not certain that Northam was one of the men, he apologized for the photograph. He managed to survive the scandal when the state's lieutenant governor and attorney general, who were in line to succeed Northam if he left office, were discovered to have scandals of their own.

Tweets from the Past

Scandals lie in wait in social media archives. A celebrity's Twitter feed, if not pruned of embarrassing material, is a fertile ground for some enterprising person to dredge up a ten-year-old tweet and set the internet on fire. In 2021 Alexi McCammond was about to take the reins as editor in chief of *Teen Vogue* magazine. Mc-Cammond, age twenty-seven, had risen rapidly to a plum position in which she could influence both fashion and politics. Then staff members at the magazine began to protest McCammond's hiring. They referred to a series of tweets that McCammond had made when she was seventeen. The tweets, which many viewed as homophobic and anti-Asian, had turned up a couple of years before, but McCammond thought her fervent apologies at the time had settled the issue. However, staff members refused to budge. They demanded that *Teen Vogue*'s parent company, Condé Nast, cut ties with her. Despite another apology, McCammond continued to trend on social media, and not in a positive way. Advertisers threatened to pull their business. It was decided that McCammond's resignation was in everyone's best interests.

Ironically, the so-called woke mob in this case had canceled a political ally. McCammond, who is Black, shared her critics' passionate belief in social justice and had intended to pursue such themes at *Teen Vogue*. "Cancel culture fundamentally preaches that forgiveness [is] impossible, and that neither time nor remorse can ever wipe away the stain of sin," says Douglas Blair, a writer with the conservative Heritage Foundation. "It didn't matter how many times McCammond apologized, nor that her offensive tweets are almost a decade old at this point, and almost certainly do not reflect who she is today."[11]

Another high-profile person to be confronted with offensive past tweets is James Gunn, director of Marvel Studios' *Guardians of the Galaxy*. In 2018 a right-wing media personality named Mike Cernovich dug up some of Gunn's tweets from nearly a decade before, featuring disturbing jokes about child abuse and other sensitive topics. Cernovich had apparently targeted Gunn for his criticism of then-president Donald Trump and Republican politicians. Pressured by the Twitter storm that ensued, Disney, the parent of Marvel Studios, fired Gunn from his next film project for the company. Gunn has since been rehired to direct films at Marvel.

Harassment with Doxing Attacks

Social media users sometimes employ even more radical means to harass people they oppose. A tactic called doxing refers to post-

A Backlash over Movie Casting

The cancel culture push for racial and gender equality can produce a tangle of competing interests. One issue that consistently draws controversy is the casting of White actors to play non-White characters in movies. Over the decades, Hollywood has frequently cast White actors to play Asian, Hispanic, or Native American roles or has changed the source materials to make the protagonists White—a practice that critics call whitewashing. Today casting decisions judged to be discriminatory or insensitive receive strong blowback on Twitter.

In 2019 actor Scarlett Johansson found herself at the center of a Twitter storm about casting. Johansson had been criticized for her role in the 2017 film *Ghost in the Shell*, based on a Japanese anime classic. In that film, a black-wigged Johansson played the main character, Major. Keith Chow, who founded the blog *The Nerds of Color*, led social media protests over the selection of a White actor to play an obviously Asian role. Johansson acknowledged that Hollywood has often favored White actors. But she went on to defend her right to play any sort of character. "I personally feel that, in an ideal world, any actor should be able to play anybody," she said, "and Art, in all forms, should be immune to political correctness."

Quoted in Tara Edwards, "Scarlett Johansson Sparks Backlash by Saying She's Allowed to Play Anything—Even a Tree," *Refinery 29*, July 14, 2019. www.refinery29.com.

ing online a person's personal information, including things such as home address and cell phone number. Victims of doxing include not only public figures but private citizens. Most social media platforms have strict rules to prevent doxing attacks and other threatening behavior. Eva Galperin, director of cybersecurity at the Electronic Frontier Foundation, says people often do not think about a doxing attack until it is too late. According to Galperin:

> The good news is that doxing is against the Terms of Service of just about every web platform I can think of. So you can report the doxing to the platform, [and] they'll usually suspend the person's account, or force them to take the post down or delete the post in question. But if you're facing really coordinated harassment, sometimes by that time it's too late, because they can amass a troll army at that point. They can keep changing platforms.[12]

Some critics on both the left and right consider dredging up old tweets or doxing individuals to be very worrisome trends. They warn that such activities can lapse into vendettas with unpredictable outcomes. Not only celebrities but ordinary people, too, can be swept up in a cancel campaign. For a private citizen, the possibility of getting fired or being threatened with doxing can bring second thoughts about sharing opinions online.

A Debate About Power

So-called cancel culture emerged from Black culture and the half-humorous idea of canceling someone whose bad behavior has gone too far. Black activists consider canceling, or rejecting a person entirely, an expression of cultural and political power among those who have lacked such power in the past. Cancel culture has generally adopted the woke sensibility of political progressives. Users on social media, especially Twitter, band together to call out hate speech or bad behavior. The trend has also generated controversy, especially among those concerned that ordinary people can be targeted with vindictive attacks online. Whatever its true impact on society, cancel culture seems certain to attract more debates about power. "Canceling is a way to acknowledge that you don't have to have the power to change structural inequality," says Anne Charity Hudley, who teaches linguistics of African America at the University of California, Santa Barbara. "You don't even have to have the power to change all of public sentiment. But as an individual, you can still have power beyond measure."[13]

> "Canceling is a way to acknowledge that you don't have to have the power to change structural inequality. You don't even have to have the power to change all of public sentiment. But as an individual, you can still have power beyond measure."[13]
>
> —Anne Charity Hudley, who teaches linguistics of African America at the University of California, Santa Barbara

CHAPTER TWO

The #MeToo Movement

In early December 2020, a tweet from an anonymous woman in Turkey set off a chain reaction of claims about sexual harassment and assault. Posting under the name "Leyla Salinger," the woman accused Hasan Ali Toptas, a well-known Turkish author, of harassing her when she was a university student. Her tweet inspired a rush of similar stories from women, about Toptas and other famous personalities. Joining together under the hashtag #MayYouLoseSleep, the victims shared harrowing accounts of harassment and assault. Many admitted that fear and shame had kept them silent for years.

The flood of accusations prompted those who were accused to respond. Toptas issued an apology on Twitter but claimed to be innocent of the charges. Others admitted to regrets for bad behavior in the past. Another of Salinger's alleged harassers, publisher Ibrahim Colak, tweeted an apology and then took his own life. Colak's suicide sparked a number of threats against the Salinger account, causing it to be shut down. However, women's groups in Turkey overwhelmingly supported the outpouring of victims' stories. They criticized the Turkish government for not providing more protection for women against sexual violence. Melis Alphan, a longtime activist for women's rights in Turkey, revealed on Twitter that a family friend had sexually harassed her when she was twenty-two. "It is not easy to talk about it," she admitted. "Even after 20 years. In the early days, I could talk about [it] but then I wanted to forget it myself. I felt better after a while. But the wounds have left behind their scars."[14]

Origins of #MeToo

Alphan and the other victims were saying, *Me too. I have been harassed like you have.* It took several years for the #MeToo movement to reach Turkey. Its male-dominated society had proved to be mostly impervious to the combination of cancel culture and claims of sexual assault and harassment. As Turkish women's rights attorney Fidan Ataselim notes, "Many men think that if they just wear a tie and utter a few words of regret, they will get away with it in court. And often it's true."[15] But as in other countries, the #MeToo push in Turkey has made a difference. Once the veil of silence was ripped away, a torrent of accusations began to pour forth.

The #MeToo movement has been one of the most visible expressions of cancel culture worldwide. The movement began in 2006, when Black activist Tarana Burke founded a nonprofit group to help survivors of sexual harassment and abuse. Burke came up with the name MeToo after listening to a thirteen-year-old survivor of sexual abuse tell her story at a youth camp. Burke realized that many females had similar stories to share.

> "Many men think that if they just wear a tie and utter a few words of regret, they will get away with it in court. And often it's true."[15]
>
> —Fidan Ataselim, a Turkish women's rights attorney

Eleven years later, Burke's efforts reached a large audience of women primed to respond. In February 2017 Uber employee Susan Fowler published a long essay about the ride-sharing company's toxic workplace culture, in which sexual harassment thrived.

The #MeToo movement has been one of the most visible expressions of cancel culture worldwide. Tarana Burke (pictured in 2019) founded the movement to help women who had suffered sexual harassment and abuse.

Fowler's story caused Uber chief executive officer (CEO) and cofounder Travis Kalanick to resign, and also led to the firing of twenty employees who had enabled the culture. In April 2017 the *New York Times* published reports about five female employees at Fox News who alleged sexual harassment by prime-time host Bill O'Reilly. Despite O'Reilly's high ratings and protests of innocence, he was fired for misconduct. The year before, Fox News CEO Roger Ailes had been forced to resign following harassment allegations by on-screen personality Gretchen Carlson and other women. And during the 2016 presidential campaign, at least a dozen women accused Republican nominee Donald Trump of rape and sexual assault. However, these developments were just rumblings of a much larger movement to come.

Weinstein and the Explosion of #MeToo

On October 5, 2017, with new concerns about sexual harassment in the air, the *New York Times* presented a bombshell exposé about one of Hollywood's most powerful figures, producer

Harvey Weinstein. The front-page story detailed allegations, spanning three decades, of Weinstein's sexual harassment. Among the alleged victims who spoke out were several actresses, including Ashley Judd and Rose McGowan, along with former employees of the Weinstein Company. Weinstein was accused of forcing women to massage him and promising to boost their careers in exchange for sexual favors.

Despite Weinstein's public apologies and partial denials, the board of his company fired him three days after the *New York Times* story appeared. That same week, the *New Yorker* magazine ran a story featuring sexual allegations about Weinstein from thirteen more women. Three of the women accused him of rape. Among the actresses claiming that Weinstein had harassed them were Mira Sorvino, Gwyneth Paltrow, and Angelina Jolie. Director Peter Jackson later reported that Weinstein had urged him not to cast Judd and Sorvino in his *Lord of the Rings* epic because they were difficult to work with.

Suddenly, a dam seemed to break. Women of all ages and various backgrounds took to Twitter and other platforms to break their silence about instances of sexual harassment and assault. Many women responded to the accounts by simply tweeting "Me Too." The hashtag #MeToo quickly went viral as shorthand for all the fear and trauma women had been hiding for years. Burke was astonished at how her phrase about shared stories had come to define a movement. But she warned that not all women were comfortable with speaking out. As Burke explained:

> We are in a time where the more you share about yourself, the more people like you; the more likes you get, the more attention on social media. . . . What we're trying to do is counter that narrative and say, "You don't have to tell your story publicly. You don't have to tell anybody what happened to you." You have to get it out—but . . . it doesn't have to be on social media at all. It could be a trusted friend. It could be your journal.[16]

A Reckoning for Sexual Offenses

The outpouring of similar stories about workplace harassment and sexual misbehavior led to real consequences. Cancel culture, in this case, left many alleged offenders genuinely canceled—with firings, forced resignations, and public shaming among the penalties. For Weinstein, the charges of rape in offices, suites, and hotel rooms kept multiplying. Eventually, more than three dozen women came forward with stories about Weinstein's sexual improprieties. He was also accused of paying large sums to actresses and employees to keep them quiet. In February 2020 the former producer was convicted of rape and sexual assault. The judge sentenced Weinstein to twenty-three years in prison. Many in Hollywood agreed that Weinstein would forever be linked to #MeToo. "We're at a watershed moment, this is a sea change," said actor Tom Hanks. "His last name . . . will become an identifying moniker for a state of being for which there was a before and an after."[17]

Following the Weinstein revelations in October 2017, the list of high-profile men accused of workplace sexual harassment and assault grew by the day. Among those fired were *Today Show* host Matt Lauer, longtime PBS talk show host Charlie Rose, comedian Louis C.K., journalist Mark Halperin, and NPR senior vice president of news Michael Oreskes. There were also men who made accusations about sexual abuse and misconduct. Actor Kevin Spacey was fired from the Netflix drama *House of Cards* after a male actor claimed he had been sexually abused at age fourteen by Spacey. Veteran Metropolitan Opera conductor James Levine faced accusations of sexual misconduct from several male musicians. After a court battle, Levine was forced out, but not before securing a $3.5 million settlement package.

> "We're at a watershed moment, this is a sea change."[17]
>
> —Tom Hanks, actor, on the #MeToo movement

Nonetheless, it was clear that positions of power and prestige no longer guaranteed protection from less-powerful accusers. A

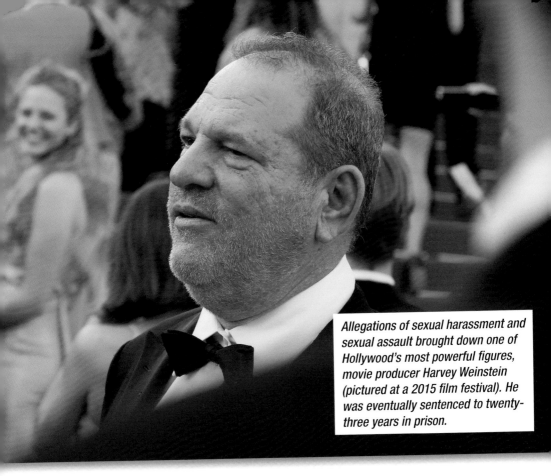

Allegations of sexual harassment and sexual assault brought down one of Hollywood's most powerful figures, movie producer Harvey Weinstein (pictured at a 2015 film festival). He was eventually sentenced to twenty-three years in prison.

perfect example was the rapid fall of billionaire casino tycoon Steve Wynn. In January 2018 the *Wall Street Journal* published an in-depth investigation revealing that, over several decades, the seventy-six-year-old Wynn had been harassing female employees and coercing them into having sex. In at least one case, he had paid $7.5 million to a former employee who had shared her story of harassment with coworkers. The news report in the *Wall Street Journal* led Wynn to step down as finance chair of the Republican National Committee. Shortly afterward, Wynn resigned as head of Wynn Resorts. He thus became the first CEO of a publicly traded company to lose his position as a result of #MeToo accusations. As many commentators noted, his accusers were individuals who once would have been ignored. They included a manicurist, a massage therapist, and a number of cocktail waitresses in Las Vegas.

#MeToo and the USA Gymnastics Women's Team

One of the most disturbing revelations from the #MeToo movement involved sexual abuse suffered by American female gymnasts. In 2016 the *Indianapolis Star* published a shocking exposé claiming that USA Gymnastics had failed to notify authorities about athletes' allegations of sexual abuse in the program. Five years later, a Federal Bureau of Investigation (FBI) watchdog report revealed that USA Gymnastics had twice notified the FBI office in Indianapolis about the allegations. At least forty female athletes had accused Larry Nassar, the team doctor for USA Gymnastics, of sexually assaulting them. Yet FBI agents took months to respond to the charges of abuse.

The *Indianapolis Star* report led to a flood of similar accusations from athletes. In all, more than three hundred athletes came forward with stories of how Nassar had sexually molested them while pretending to offer treatment. Among the accusers were America's top Olympic gymnasts, including Simone Biles, Aly Raisman, Gabby Douglas, and McKayla Maroney. After a sensational trial in which many of the victims testified, Nassar was sentenced to life in prison. "Imagine feeling like you have no power and no voice," Raisman said in court testimony. "Well, you know what, Larry? I have both power and voice, and I am only just beginning to use them."

Quoted in Carla Correa, "The #MeToo Moment: For U.S. Gymnasts, Why Did Justice Take So Long?," *New York Times*, January 25, 2018. www.nytimes.com.

Painful Accusations and Repeated Denials

The #MeToo movement brought to light painful accusations that went back decades. Such was the case with filmmaker Woody Allen. In March 2020 Allen made news with the publication of his memoir. The book detailed his prolific career as a writer and director, during which he has made nearly fifty films. But the news reports could not ignore another aspect of the story. In his book, Allen once more denied accusations by his adopted daughter Dylan Farrow, alleging that he sexually abused her when she was seven years old. Farrow's accusations date to the 1990s, and several police investigations at that time failed to establish that the abuse occurred. Nonetheless, Allen's reputation plummeted.

In the age of #MeToo and cancel culture, his reputation has taken further hits. In March 2020 Hachette Book Group, Allen's original publisher, decided not to publish his memoir after its staff walked out in protest. Other major firms also rejected the book, although Allen finally found another publisher. Meanwhile, Amazon Prime canceled a four-movie contract with the director, and several major stars said they regretted having appeared in his films. However, director Spike Lee, a longtime friend, came to Allen's defense on a New York radio show. "I'd just like to say Woody Allen is a great, great filmmaker, and this cancel thing is not just Woody," Lee declared. "And I think when we look back on it we are going to see that—short of killing somebody—I don't know that you can just erase somebody like they never existed."[18]

Lee's testimonial quickly brought a storm of Twitter outrage down on his own head. In response, he tweeted an apology: "I Deeply Apologize. My Words Were WRONG. I Do Not And Will Not Tolerate Sexual Harassment, Assault or Violence. Such Treatment Causes Real Damage That Can't Be Minimized.—Truly, Spike Lee."[19]

As for Allen, Amazon Prime eventually returned his latest films to its website. In 2021 the director began making his fiftieth film in Paris, with European actors.

The Kavanaugh Hearings and #BelieveWomen

As #MeToo proceeded, another hashtag was added to the movement: #BelieveWomen. Feminists argued that too often in the past a woman's accusations about sexual harassment and assault tended to be dismissed as untrue or an overreaction. They urged that women's claims be given due consideration. It was clear that making accusations against powerful men was not done lightly. Such a step required courage and often came with a large personal cost, requiring the accuser to relive an agonizing memory. Polls at the time showed that Americans generally agreed with the idea behind #BelieveWomen. They were more concerned about men getting away with sexual assault or harassment than with them being victimized by false allegations.

Believing women is much easier when a number of victims come forward with similar stories about harassment, as in the Weinstein case. But things get murkier when there is only one accuser and the alleged perpetrator has no known history of sexual misconduct. Lawyers call it the "she said–he said" dilemma, and it makes the truth very difficult to determine.

In September 2018 this dilemma played out before the nation with very high stakes: the confirmation of a Supreme Court justice. In the middle of Senate hearings vetting Judge Brett Kavanaugh, Trump's nominee for the high court, a serious charge surfaced. Christine Blasey Ford, a psychology professor in California, claimed that a drunken Kavanaugh had sexually assaulted her at a party in the 1980s, when both were in high school. Ford's therapist testified that Ford had mentioned the incident in one of her sessions in 2012. Ford's emotional testimony before the Senate Judiciary Committee, which was televised live, was compelling. She told the committee:

> I truly wish I could provide detailed answers to all of the questions that have been and will be asked about how I got to the party, where it took place, and so forth. I don't have all the answers, and I don't remember as much as I would like to. But the details about that night that bring me here today are ones I will never forget. They have been seared into my memory and have haunted me episodically as an adult.[20]

Ford's testimony convinced many observers that she was telling the truth. Others disagreed, noting that she could not recall the date and location of the party and that there were no witnesses to the alleged assault. Kavanaugh's defenders insisted he was being attacked unfairly with vague charges from when he was a teenager. Reactions mostly were split along partisan lines, as expected in such a politically fraught situation.

A "he said-she said" scenario played out during the 2018 Senate confirmation hearing of Judge Brett Kavanaugh, a nominee for the US Supreme Court. Psychology professor Christine Blasey Ford (pictured) testified that Kavanaugh had sexually assaulted her at a party in the 1980s when both were in high school.

The following day, when Kavanaugh returned to testify, he angrily denied Ford's charges, along with those of two much less credible accusers. There were also a number of wilder accusations, including tales of gang rapes, that had circulated in recent days. "This confirmation process has become a national disgrace," Kavanaugh declared to the committee. "The constitution gives the Senate an important role in the confirmation process, but you have replaced advice and consent with search and destroy."[21] Despite all the fireworks, the full Senate voted to approve Kavanaugh as a Supreme Court justice. But the battle had raised new questions across the political spectrum about #MeToo, unproven claims, and cancel culture.

The Limits of #MeToo

Progressives have touted the success of #MeToo in bringing accountability to long-ignored habits of sexual harassment in the

The Impact of #MeToo on Campus

When #MeToo emerged, it built on past efforts by the Barack Obama administration to address sexual harassment and sexual assault on America's campuses. In 2011 the US Department of Education had sent a letter to schools that provided guidance on how administrators should handle allegations of sexual harassment or assault. The "Dear Colleague" letter required more than seven thousand colleges that receive federal funding to use the lowest possible standard of proof—called preponderance of evidence—in deciding on-campus cases of sexual assault. The letter also limited cross-examining of accusers and allowed accusers to appeal findings of not guilty. All this was justified as part of Title IX's mission to end discrimination against females on campus.

Republicans contended that the change stacked the deck against males accused of a sex offense on campus. In 2017 Betsy DeVos, secretary of education under Donald Trump, announced a new rule to require due process reforms for campus sexual-assault cases. For example, students accused of sexual assault would be able to cross-examine witnesses, including their accusers. DeVos's rule passed muster with federal judges. But after Joe Biden won the White House in 2020, new education secretary Miguel Cardona announced plans to overturn DeVos's changes. As a result, #MeToo continues to spur a tug-of-war on campuses.

workplace. In October 2018 the *New York Times* reported that #MeToo had helped bring down 201 powerful men who were guilty of harassment or assault. Plus, said the newspaper, nearly half of those offenders had been replaced by women. And there were other positive effects. A 2019 study conducted by Yale University and the Tobin Center for Economic Policy found that #MeToo had helped increase reporting of sex crimes overall by 14 percent worldwide and by 7 percent in the United States.

However, an accusation on the presidential campaign trail in April 2020 threatened to splinter progressive support for the #MeToo movement and #BelieveWomen. Tara Reade, a former Senate aide, claimed that Joe Biden, the Democratic nominee for president, had assaulted her in 1993 and that she had shared her story with others at the time. Biden's campaign denied the allegation, while former members of his Senate staff said they had never heard about such an incident.

Republicans, including Trump, were eager to hold Democrats to their commitment to believe women's stories about sexual abuse. They pointed out that Biden himself had voiced public support for Christine Blasey Ford after her Senate committee appearance. Meanwhile, Democrats like House Speaker Nancy Pelosi defended Biden while also affirming their basic allegiance to #MeToo. And with so many accusations swirling about Trump himself, Democrats leveled their own charges of hypocrisy. Moreover, progressives said the movement never intended that women should always be believed in all circumstances. Yet many commentators came to acknowledge that, for all its healthy effects, #MeToo had to have limits. According to *New York Times* opinion columnist Maureen Dowd, "To suggest that every woman who alleges a sexual assault is as credible as the next is absurd. The idea that no woman can ever be wrong just hurts women. . . . Democrats always set standards that come back and bite them. They have created a cage of their own making."[22]

> "To suggest that every woman who alleges a sexual assault is as credible as the next is absurd. The idea that no woman can ever be wrong just hurts women."[22]
>
> —Maureen Dowd, *New York Times* opinion columnist

In any event, some of the momentum of the #MeToo movement has given way to a more cautious attitude. Activists still want women's claims of sexual abuse to be taken seriously. But more observers are insisting that accusations be supported with evidence as well.

CHAPTER THREE

Cancel Culture and Political Speech

In recent political battles in the United States, both sides often accuse each other of having lost their minds. In January 2020 a psychiatry professor at Yale University lost her job over just such a claim. Her remarks came in a Twitter discussion about Trump lawyer Alan Dershowitz. The professor, Dr. Bandy Lee, said that "given the severity and spread of 'shared psychosis' among just about all of Trump's followers" it was likely that Dershowitz "has wholly taken on Trump's symptoms by contagion."[23] Many of Lee's followers promptly tweeted their agreement.

However, Dershowitz protested in a letter to Yale faculty. He noted that Lee, a psychiatrist, had publicly diagnosed him as psychotic, without examining him and based entirely on his political views. According to Dershowitz, this was a clear violation of the American Psychiatric Association's rules on ethics. Dr. John Krystal, chair of the Yale Department of Psychiatry, agreed. He said that Lee had violated professional conduct and warned her about further violations. In May 2020 she received notice of her firing. A little more than a year later, Lee filed suit against Yale, claiming she was wrongly terminated for exercising her right of free speech. In an email to the Yale newspaper, Lee explained her legal action. "I have done this with a heavy heart, only because Yale refused all my requests for a discussion," she said. "I love Yale, my alma mater, as I love my country, but we are falling into a dangerous culture of self-censorship and compliance with authority at all cost."[24]

> "I love Yale, my alma mater, as I love my country, but we are falling into a dangerous culture of self-censorship and compliance with authority at all cost."[24]
>
> —Dr. Bandy Lee, psychiatry professor at Yale University

Campus Canceling Based on Politics

More than a few teachers and administrators, including many conservatives, would agree with Lee's assessment of campus culture. They worry that expressing opinions that offend the dom-

Lawyer Alan Dershowitz (speaking at a 2019 White House gathering) persuaded Yale University to fire a psychiatry professor who had tweeted about Dershowitz's state of mind in supporting and representing Donald Trump.

inant woke viewpoint will lead to professional trouble. Dr. Stephen Hsu, a physicist and administrator at Michigan State University (MSU), provides a recent example. Hsu first came under fire for tweets and blog posts that expressed his conservative views. In one post from 2018, he wrote, "We are scientists, seeking truth. We are not slaves to ideological conformity."[25] On June 10, 2020, members of MSU's Graduate Employees Union engaged in a long Twitter thread that condemned Hsu. Some tweets claimed that Hsu was a racist. The group criticized his role in funding a controversial study of bias in police shootings. The study, conducted by MSU psychologist Joe Cesario, found that officers were not more prone to shoot when dealing with a Black suspect than a White suspect. On June 11 a petition signed by hundreds of MSU students and employees demanded that Hsu be fired.

At first, MSU's president defended Hsu. The university released a statement in support of its faculty's rights to academic freedom. But as the controversy swelled, the tide turned against Hsu. Two weeks later, he was asked to resign his administrative post. Cesario saw Hsu's termination as an alarming sign. It's "bad or worse that they are doing this to an administrator," said Cesario. "If anybody should be allowed to explore all topics, speak on all topics, and go where the data leads them, it's administrators." Cesario added

> "If anybody should be allowed to explore all topics, speak on all topics, and go where the data leads them, it's [college] administrators."[26]
>
> —Joe Cesario, Michigan State University psychologist and researcher

that the activists who got Hsu dismissed probably will not stop "pushing for a narrowing of what kinds of topics people can talk about, or what kinds of conclusions people can come to."[26]

Some argue that outspoken educators invite the backlash and that cancel culture is simply calling out their offensive views. In June 2020 David Collum, a longtime chemistry professor at Cornell University, was blasted for a tweet that seemed to defend police brutality. A viral video shot during a Black Lives Matter protest

An All-Star Cancellation

When politics collides with professional sports, whole cities can get canceled. In 2021 the city of Atlanta, Georgia, was preparing to host an historic Major League Baseball (MLB) All-Star Game in July. Not only would the city welcome the best ballplayers in the world, it would also present an emotional tribute to Hank Aaron, the Hall of Fame slugger who had recently died. Aaron had broken Babe Ruth's all-time home run record in Atlanta as a longtime member of the Braves.

However, the Atlanta All-Star Game and the hometown tribute to Aaron were not to be. On April 2, 2021, MLB commissioner Rob Manfred announced that the game was being pulled from Atlanta. The decision was reached after the Republican-led Georgia legislature passed an election bill that opponents, including President Biden, claimed made voting more difficult for people of color. As Atlanta mayor Keisha Lance Bottoms tweeted, "Unfortunately, the removal of the @MLB All Star game from GA is likely the 1st of many dominoes to fall, until the unnecessary barriers put in place to restrict access to the ballot box are removed." Republicans protested that MLB was taking political sides. In response to MLB's move, many conservative fans swore to boycott the remainder of the season.

Quoted in Todd Haselton, "MLB Pulls 2021 All-Star Game Out of Atlanta Due to Georgia's New Restrictive Voting Law," CNBC, April 2, 2021. www.cnbc.com.

in Buffalo, New York, showed two officers shoving an elderly White protester to the pavement. The man lay bleeding from his head as the police filed past him. Later reports revealed that the protester had suffered a cracked skull. In response to the video, Collum tweeted, "That guy needed to give that cop space. Wasn't brutality: the guy was feeble. The cracked skull . . . was self inflicted."[27] Angered by Collum's tweet, Cornell students swiftly gathered four thousand signatures on a petition demanding his termination. Under fire for this and for past statements, Collum was forced to step down. Cornell president Martha E. Pollack made clear that she considered the professor's tweet to be deeply offensive. "While Professor Collum has a right to express his views in his private life," she said, "we also have a right and an obligation to call out positions that are at direct odds with Cornell's ethos."[28] Still, some conservative pundits questioned whether personal opinions deserved such professional punishment.

Diverging Views on Cancel Culture

Surveys show that liberals and conservatives differ a great deal in their views of cancel culture on campus. A survey of political science professors, published by Harvard University's Pippa Norris, director of the Electoral Integrity Project, found that left-leaning professors do not consider cancel culture a major problem. Conservatives disagree, finding it a significant issue. The conservative columnist Jeff Jacoby argues that college campuses feature less diversity of opinion every year, with left-wing opinions dominating.

To navigate the political minefields of cancel culture, non-progressives say they must resort to self-censorship. Right-leaning academics generally try to avoid controversy by keeping their political opinions to themselves. In February 2020 the *Atlantic* reported that conservative students on campus also feel pressured to hide their views. Perhaps surprisingly, their concerns did not center on teachers, whom they mostly judged to be impartial in classroom discussions and grading. Instead, nearly one-quarter said they feared being "outed" by woke classmates for expressing conservative opinions. Campus speech codes can present another minefield. Designed to regulate hate speech such as racist, sexist, or demeaning language, they sometimes go further to discourage political speech that mocks or ridicules opposing viewpoints.

Self-censorship extends beyond the American campus. An August 2020 opinion poll from the Cato Institute found that 62 percent of Americans say the current political climate prevents them from stating their beliefs for fear of offending others. More than 77 percent of Republicans admitted they self-censored, compared to 52 percent of Democrats. Critics of cancel culture contend that both percentages are too high for a society dedicated to free speech.

In-House Cancel Culture at the *New York Times*

Political battle lines have brought cancel culture to the news media in some high-profile cases. Efforts to present all sides of an issue can land editors in trouble with those who see opposition views as hateful or beyond the pale. Such a situation occurred during the George Floyd protests in the summer of 2020. As some protests grew violent and destructive in major cities, conservatives called for stronger measures to stop the rioting. To explore this argument, *New York Times* opinion editor James Bennet published a controversial op-ed piece by Arkansas senator Tom Cotton. The editorial, titled "Send in the Troops," appeared on June 3, 2020. In it Cotton urged the Trump administration to deploy military troops in cities where protests had turned violent. Cotton argued that elites were making excuses for the rioters and looters, who were undermining peaceful protests. He also contended that police officers around the nation were bearing the worst of the violence.

Cotton's op-ed set off a firestorm of outrage, inside and outside the *New York Times*'s editorial offices. Readers questioned why the *New York Times* was giving the conservative Cotton a

An opinion piece about the violence that occurred at some of the 2020 Black Lives Matter protests sparked an outcry. Calls for the firing of the New York Times editor who had allowed its publication led to the editor's resignation.

forum. The newspaper's staff members condemned the piece on Twitter and claimed that it endangered the lives of Black journalists at the paper. Bennet found himself at the center of the controversy. In another Twitter thread, Bennet explained that he owed it to *New York Times* readers to offer counterarguments to the paper's pro-protest editorials. "We understand that many readers find Senator Cotton's argument painful, even dangerous," Bennet wrote. "We believe that is one reason it requires public scrutiny and debate."[29]

Nonetheless, the calls for Bennet to be fired only increased. The newspaper's management printed an apology, saying the editing process had been rushed and as a result the piece did not meet *New York Times* standards. Stories circulated that Bennet had not read Cotton's op-ed before publishing it. On June 7 Bennet was forced to resign.

Canceling the President

Former president Donald Trump has recognized few limits on expressing his views, including before, during, and after his turbulent four years in office. Since joining Twitter in 2009, Trump had amassed more than 88.9 million followers. His near-daily tweets during the 2016 election campaign and throughout his presidency sparked extreme reactions from his fans and detractors alike. Despite Trump's personal attacks and promotion of conspiracy theories, Twitter was generally reluctant to regulate his messages in any way.

Yet tensions grew between Trump and the social media companies, especially Twitter. In October 2019 Twitter announced a new policy aimed at world leaders—including Trump. A tweet judged to be false or misleading would not be removed but instead placed behind a warning so that users would have to click through to read it. But in May 2020, after Twitter added fact-check warnings to a pair of his tweets, Trump threatened (ironically, via a tweet) to shut down social media platforms. "Republicans feel that Social Media Platforms totally silence conservative voices,"

A Republican Rebel Gets Canceled

Conservatives often see themselves as the chief victims of cancel culture. Yet they can wield their own cancellation axes when they choose. On May 12, 2021, House Republicans removed Wyoming representative Liz Cheney from her House leadership role. The move was aimed at punishing Cheney for her rejection of former president Trump and his claims of election fraud in the 2020 presidential election.

The meeting of House Republicans to select the party's leadership, held behind closed doors quickly became raucous. Instead of fighting to save her position, Cheney delivered a defiant speech. She warned her fellow party members that they risked destruction if they continued to silence dissent and pretend that the election was stolen. Cheney's final words were drowned out by a chorus of boos. Her ouster came so quickly that some Republicans were still arriving when the voice vote concluded. As Colorado Republican Ken Buck said afterward, "Liz didn't agree with President Trump's narrative, and she was canceled."

Quoted in Catie Edmondson and Nicholas Fandos, "Republicans Oust a Defiant Cheney, Confirming Trump's Grasp on the Party," *New York Times*, May 12, 2021. www.nytimes.com.

Trump tweeted. "We will strongly regulate, or close them down, before we can ever allow this to happen."[30]

Following the Capitol riot by his supporters on January 6, 2021, Trump was hit with a form of cancellation that raised new controversy about speech platforms and free expression. In a speech on January 6, Trump had urged a large crowd of his supporters to march to the Capitol to protest what he claimed was a stolen election. Subsequently, hundreds of Trump supporters forced their way into the Capitol, vandalized the premises, and fought for hours with police in an attempt to stop the official certification of the election results. Some of the rioters threatened violence against Vice President Mike Pence and members of Congress. The riot shocked the nation and was widely condemned by Democrats and some Republicans. On January 9 Twitter announced that Trump was permanently banned from the platform due to the risk of his inciting further violence. All at once, the leader of the free world had lost his chief means of instantaneous communication with 88 million followers—his so-called megaphone to the nation.

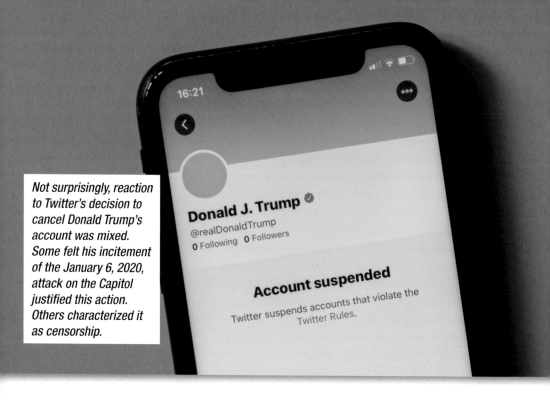

16:21

<

Donald J. Trump ✓
@realDonaldTrump
0 Following 0 Followers

Account suspended

Twitter suspends accounts that violate the
Twitter Rules.

Not surprisingly, reaction to Twitter's decision to cancel Donald Trump's account was mixed. Some felt his incitement of the January 6, 2020, attack on the Capitol justified this action. Others characterized it as censorship.

Trump's political opponents welcomed this momentous step. But for his supporters, the Twitter ban seemed to vindicate Trump's warnings about the sweeping power and partisanship of social media companies. Many world leaders reacted with alarm. They blasted Twitter's decision as one that should have been left to the American people, not a private company. German chancellor Angela Merkel called the move problematic, while acting Australian prime minister Michael McCormack referred to it as censorship. Mexican president Andrés Manuel López Obrador worried about the digital might of social media. "I don't like anybody being censored or taking away from the right to post a message on Twitter or Facebook," said López Obrador. "I don't agree with that, I don't accept that. . . . This is really serious."[31] In June 2021 Facebook also banned Trump from its platform for at least two years. In doing this, Facebook's oversight board was upholding a suspension that dated from the day after the Capitol riot. Nonetheless, as many observers have noted, the former president has not been silenced. He continues to draw huge crowds at rallies and share his opinions with followers via interviews and blog posts.

When Political Attacks Become Personal

Public figures like Trump are used to the rough-and-tumble nature of political disputes. But cancel culture can be unnerving for those not used to the vitriol. Twenty-one-year-old Wilson Gavin, a gay student and Young Liberal in Brisbane, Australia, faced a social media onslaught when he led a protest against a drag performer reading to children at the Brisbane Square Library. Gavin believed the event was inappropriate for young children. When a video of the protest went viral, Twitter exploded with personal attacks on Gavin. A few days later, he took his own life.

Some targets, however, are able to fight back. In January 2019 Nicholas Sandmann, a seventeen-year-old from Kentucky, received a roasting on Twitter due to a posted video. The video showed him apparently confronting Nathan Phillips, a Native American elder and activist who was beating a small drum at close quarters. Sandmann, part of a youth group attending a March for Life in Washington, DC, was wearing a bright red MAGA hat, which seemed to infuriate his Twitter critics. They decided that Sandmann's smile showed that he was mocking Phillips. One said he would like to punch Sandmann in the face. When an American Civil Liberties Union employee revealed where Sandmann planned to attend college, several tweets demanded that the school refuse his enrollment. Overall, Twitter, TV pundits, and news reporters seemed to characterize Sandmann as a privileged and insensitive young Trump supporter.

> "I don't like anybody being censored or taking away from the right to post a message on Twitter or Facebook. I don't agree with that, I don't accept that. . . . This is really serious."[31]
>
> —Andrés Manuel López Obrador, Mexican president, on Trump's Twitter ban

Within days, an unedited version of the video emerged. It showed that Sandmann and the other students had been showered with profane taunts by a Black protest group. And Phillips had approached Sandmann, not the other way around. Conservative editors sprang to Sandmann's defense. They pointed out that he was not even an adult and had been attacked unfairly before all the facts were known. Sandmann's family eventually filed suit against several media outlets for defamation. CNN and the *Washington Post* both settled out of court for undisclosed sums.

In a time of severe political divisions, people on both the left and right have fallen victim to cancel culture. Some teachers and administrators on American campuses find they must be wary of offending others on Twitter when making public statements or conducting controversial research. Some professors admit to self-censorship on campus in order to avoid professional trouble. Threats of cancellation over politics can strike everyone from high-profile news editors to the president of the United States. They can also intimidate private citizens unused to the spotlight. As former president Barack Obama said in October 2019,

"There is this sense sometimes of: 'The way of me making change is to be as judgmental as possible about other people and that's enough.' . . . That's not activism. That's not bringing about change. If all you're doing is casting stones, you're probably not going to get that far."[32]

—Barack Obama, former US president

"Among certain young people, and this is accelerated by social media, there is this sense sometimes of: 'The way of me making change is to be as judgmental as possible about other people and that's enough.' . . . That's not activism. That's not bringing about change. If all you're doing is casting stones, you're probably not going to get that far."[32]

CHAPTER FOUR

Reexamining the Past

After 9/11, the New York Yankees and other MLB teams switched out the seventh-inning singalong of "Take Me Out to the Ballgame" for "God Bless America." Occasionally, the teams would have live singers. But the most popular rendition of the Irving Berlin classic was Kate Smith's 1938 recording. Some fans considered it practically a second national anthem. In fact, the Philadelphia Flyers hockey team had played Smith's rendition at Flyers home games since the late 1960s. The team had even erected a statue of Smith outside its arena. The singer, who died in 1986, was considered a good luck charm for the home team.

In 2019 Smith's patriotic recording ran afoul of cancel culture. A fan's email told the Yankees that in the 1930s Smith had recorded two songs with racially offensive lyrics about Blacks. The Yankees immediately decided to ditch Smith's recording. Other teams quickly did the same. The Flyers covered up Smith's statue at once and then removed it. Within days, Kate Smith had been canceled from the American landscape. Debate over Smith's banning raged on editorial pages and in letters to the editors. Defenders of the ban noted that the demeaning songs and lyrics reflected American society's racist attitudes and those who performed them deserved to be rejected. Others, however, argued that the offensive songs had not been played in public, or even noticed, for decades. And Smith herself had repudiated racism in interviews. Some wondered at the wisdom of judging the past by the political standards of today. As the *New York Daily News* asked, "Is contemporary 'wokeness' the best measure to assess the hearts and minds of performers 80 years ago?"[33]

> "Is contemporary 'wokeness' the best measure to assess the hearts and minds of performers 80 years ago?"[33]
>
> —*New York Daily News* editorial board

After the 9/11 attacks, Kate Smith's 1938 recording of "God Bless America" became a fan favorite at New York Yankees baseball games. The team dropped the song after it learned that Smith (pictured in 1975) had recorded two songs with offensive lyrics about Blacks.

A Reexamination of America's Past

In line with the political engagement of cancel culture, there has been a drive to reexamine America's past. Concerns about racism and social justice have sparked discussions about the difficult history of race relations in America and how it affects all racial groups today. Black Lives Matter and other groups have called for the removal of public symbols of slavery, segregation, and race hatred. Supporters believe this reexamination is long overdue. From issues of police violence to voting rights to economic inequality, they seek to emphasize how change is still urgently needed. Opponents, while acknowledging that much work remains to be done, claim that the protests and cancellations tend to ignore the great progress America has made in race relations, including through the historic civil rights movement of the 1960s. This disagreement tended to produce raw nerves and angry rhetoric on all sides.

Among the protesters' first targets were statues and monuments to Confederate military figures. Hundreds of these statues are found in southern states that fought on the side of the proslavery Confederacy in the Civil War. For years critics have questioned why statues honoring those who committed treason against the US government are still displayed on public lands. During the protests following George Floyd's death, protesters sometimes doused such monuments with red paint, scrawled antiracist messages on them, or joined together to pull them down. President Joe Biden has said that Confederate statues belong in museums, to be studied for the history behind them, and not in town squares. But he added that he understood the pain that such monuments could produce. "Don't be surprised if someone pulls down the statue of Jefferson Davis," Biden said in June 2020, referring to the president of the short-lived Confederacy. "It's better that they do not. . . . It's always better to do it peacefully."[34]

On July 10, 2021, one of the most divisive Confederate monuments in the country was finally lifted off its stone pedestal and hauled away. The statue of General Robert E. Lee on horseback

In July 2021 workers in Charlottesville, Virginia, remove a statue of Confederate general Robert E. Lee. The statue's removal follows years of contention, community anguish, and legal fights.

had stood in Market Street Park in Charlottesville, Virginia, since 1924. Dozens of onlookers cheered as workers hoisted the statue for removal. A statue of another Confederate leader, General Thomas "Stonewall" Jackson, was also removed. A Black high school student named Zyahna Bryant had launched the petition to remove the monuments in 2016. Seeing the statues finally hauled off left Bryant, who is now a student at the University of Virginia, with a feeling of satisfaction. "This is well overdue," she said. "No platform for white supremacy. No platform for racism. No platform for hate."[35]

Bryant was referring to a violent rally that took place in the park on August 12, 2017. Protests over plans to remove the Lee monument led to a Unite the Right rally. Far right-wing neo-Nazi and

White supremacist groups faced off against antiracist counterprotesters. In the melee that ensued, a White supremacist plowed his truck into the opposition group, killing a young woman. Nineteen other protesters were hospitalized, and two police officers died

in a helicopter crash on their way to the scene. For many Charlottesville residents, removing the Lee monument nearly four years later represented a long-awaited reckoning for the violence.

Canceling American History

But the push to eliminate politically offensive monuments did not end with Confederate statues. In remarks following the Charlottesville riot, President Trump suggested that major figures from American history might be the next targets. Their enormous accomplishments, he warned, could be forgotten in a skewed focus on their flaws. "George Washington was a slave owner. So will George Washington lose his status? Are we gonna take down statues to George Washington?" Trump asked. "How about Thomas Jefferson? . . . Do you like him, because he was a major slave owner. Are we gonna take down his statue?"[36] Trump's statements were ridiculed at the time as being frivolous and alarmist. Historians, while admitting that the debate about historical figures was ongoing, dismissed the notion that cancel culture might target America's founders.

Nonetheless, efforts to do just that soon emerged. Following the events in Charlottesville, a New Orleans–based grassroots organization called Take 'Em Down NOLA pressured New Orleans officials to take down not only Confederate statues and signs but also those of US presidents who owned slaves or oppressed minority groups. "Our position is, we don't want in your public spaces any slave masters or Confederates, those are people who should not be venerated," says Malcolm Suber, one of the

Gone with the Wind in Context

Gone with the Wind, a 1939 film set in the South during and after the Civil War, is one of the most popular movies of all time. But in the age of cancel culture, the film has come under new scrutiny. Its portrayal of slavery and African Americans in the Confederacy, say many critics, virtually ignores the hardships and cruelty that enslaved people faced. Black characters in the film are now widely seen as stereotypes, even though Hattie McDaniel, who plays a beloved housemaid, won the first Oscar by a Black actor for her performance. In June 2020 HBO Max responded to nationwide protests over the death of George Floyd by removing *Gone with the Wind* from its film library.

The decision drew criticism for judging a work from decades ago by contemporary standards. However, the announced move was only temporary. When HBO Max returned *Gone with the Wind* to its rotation, it added a disclaimer about the film's historical inaccuracies and stereotypes. According to Oscar-winning screenwriter John Ridley, "The movie had the very best talents in Hollywood at that time working together to sentimentalize a history that never was."

Quoted in Frank Pallotta, "'Gone with the Wind' Pulled from HBO Max Until It Can Return with 'Historical Context,'" CNN Business, June 10, 2020. www.cnn.com.

group's founding members. "We have always understood what these statues stood for."[37] Suber mentioned Washington and Andrew Jackson as presidents whose monuments should be removed. As president, Jackson presided over the forced relocation of thousands of Native Americans.

Four years later, in the demonstrations that followed the killing of George Floyd in Minneapolis, protesters brought down or vandalized many statues and monuments across the nation. Among the statues under attack were many Confederate figures, as well as those of Washington, Jefferson, Abraham Lincoln, and Black abolitionist Frederick Douglass. In Richmond, Virginia, a statue of explorer Christopher Columbus was yanked from its pedestal, dragged across a street, and dumped into a shallow pond. Many monuments were doused with red paint and scribbled with protest slogans. In their zeal to tear down statues, some protesters were seriously injured. Meanwhile, cities took action to remove memorials now thought to be offensive. In June 2020 Boston officials voted to remove a replica of the Emancipation Memorial in the city's Park Square. The monument depicts Lincoln standing over a kneeling Black man, exhorting him to rise. The original, which dates to 1876 and is located in Washington, DC, was paid for by freed slaves.

A Nation Divided

As the removals—and the vandalism—continued, they divided the nation further. Historians explained that attacks on statues and monuments were not unusual in periods of political upheaval. For example, American colonists had toppled statues of Britain's King George III in a prelude to the American Revolution. During the French Revolution in the 1790s, crowds destroyed statues, monuments, paintings, and other artworks that paid tribute to royalty, the Roman Catholic Church, and feudal beliefs. After the fall of the Soviet Union in 1991, Russians pulled down dozens of statues of the communist leaders Vladimir Lenin and Joseph Stalin.

Many on the left tended to view the destruction of offensive statues as a natural response to the racial tensions inflamed by Floyd's death. Writers empathized with people's deep emotional response. As *Washington Post* art critic Sebastian Smee noted, "If, as an African American, you are out with your kids or walking to work, why should you have to pass by a giant statue of Robert E. Lee—a man who led the fight to maintain the enslavement of your people? Why should the city—your city, where you pay taxes—be planting flower beds around such a statue?"[38]

Many conservatives, however, believed that the vandalism of statues and monuments had gone beyond righteous anger at

"If, as an African American, you are out with your kids or walking to work, why should you have to pass by a giant statue of Robert E. Lee—a man who led the fight to maintain the enslavement of your people?"[38]

—Sebastian Smee, art critic for the *Washington Post*

symbols of racism. Instead, it had become an assault on America itself. They deplored the lawlessness and destruction of public property. On June 26, 2020, Trump signed an executive order mandating prison sentences of up to ten years for people who tore down or vandalized statues and other historical monuments. A few months after taking office, Biden reversed Trump's order.

A Controversy over Names

The push to remove monuments to Confederate soldiers and politicians extended to America's military bases. Ten major army bases in the South were named for Confederate generals. Among them are Fort Bragg in Fayetteville, North Carolina, named for General Braxton Bragg, and Fort Hood in Killeen, Texas, named for General John Bell Hood. Fort Lee, a logistics and leadership training base located near Petersburg, Virginia, bears the name of the main Confederate commander, Robert E. Lee. With Con-federate symbols disappearing all across the South—including at auto races run by NASCAR, which in June 2020 banned the display of Confederate flags at its events—renaming these mili-tary bases seemed an inevitable next step. In May 2021 a com-mission made up of retired military commanders and experts on military affairs announced a plan to rename the ten installations. The plan was submitted for the approval of new defense secre-tary Lloyd Austin. Congress created the renaming commission as part of the 2021 National Defense Authorization Act. There has been talk of renaming at least some of the bases for distinguished Black or female military figures.

For many Black service members in particular, creating a plan to rename the bases was long overdue. In 2015, after a White supremacist murdered Black churchgoers in Charleston, South Carolina, there was a similar push to change the base names. At that time, Pentagon officials opposed the idea. But six years later support had grown considerably. Maryland representative Anthony Brown, an African American who is also a retired army colonel, has pursued the issue as vice chair of the House Armed

Confederate flags fly in the infield as cars come out of a turn during a 2007 NASCAR race at Talladega Superspeedway in Alabama. In June 2020 NASCAR banned the display of Confederate flags at its events.

Services Committee. "Bases that continue to bear the names of Confederate soldiers and officers—persons who wrongly fought to protect the institution of slavery and would have denied black Americans from serving in the military—are a reminder of that systemic oppression we continue to confront,"[39] says Brown. As Iraq War veteran Fred Wellman adds, "We are forcing our black soldiers to serve on a base named after leaders who served to keep them in chains."[40]

Despite bipartisan agreement in Congress to pursue the name changes, opinions about the issue continue to be closely divided. An ABC News–Ipsos poll in June 2020 found that 56 percent of Americans opposed changing the names of military bases named for Confederate commanders. Nearly 70 percent

Canceling Section 230

Individuals on both the left and right worry about social media firms employing their own version of cancel culture. Facebook, Twitter, YouTube, Instagram, and other platforms reserve the right to remove posts or other material they deem to be offensive or misleading. Users who are flagged can be banned for a short time or have their accounts frozen. Repeated offenses can result in a permanent ban.

Social media companies are shielded from legal liability by a part of US law referred to as Section 230. This section of the Communications Decency Act of 1996 actually is designed to protect online speech. It ensures that platforms like Twitter and Facebook can host content posted by users without being responsible for it as a publisher. Today, however, both Republicans and Democrats are considering changes to Section 230, although for different reasons. Republicans want to fight alleged censorship of conservative users. Democrats believe the platforms should be more aggressive in taking down alleged misinformation. "[Section 230] should be revoked because [Facebook] is not merely an internet company," said President Biden with regard to vaccine misinformation. "It is propagating falsehoods they know to be false. . . . It's irresponsible."

Quoted in Bryan Pietsch, "Trump and Biden Both Want to Revoke Section 230, but for Different Reasons," Business Insider, May 30, 2020. www.businessinsider.com.

of Black Americans supported the renamings, as did 54 percent of Hispanic Americans.

Renamings at Yale

Other institutions in America also have moved to rename sections associated with slavery and racism. In February 2017 Yale University removed the name of John C. Calhoun from one of its residential colleges. As a senator and then vice president before the Civil War, Calhoun was a fierce defender of slavery and states' rights. Yale renamed the college for Grace Murray Hopper, who earned advanced degrees at Yale in the 1930s prior to her breakthrough work in computing. In June 2020 Princeton University announced it was removing former president Woodrow Wilson's name from its prestigious school of public policy. A school statement noted that the change was due to Wilson's racist views and policies, including resegregating the civil service.

Calls also arose for an even larger name change at Yale. Critics attacked the legacy of Elihu Yale, the school's founder, who allegedly had profited from the slave trade during his years with the East India Company. A #CancelYale campaign trended on Twitter, fueled in part by right-wing trolls seeking to make a point about cancel culture. They wanted to show that, by the logic of cancel culture, Yale should change its prestigious name to erase its connections to racism and the slave trade. However, certain activists on the left, like Yale Law School graduate Nathan Robinson, joined the debate. "If we believe in renaming military bases that were named in honor of Confederate generals, what principled argument is there for not renaming Yale University?" said Robinson. "What principles do we use to evaluate what should and shouldn't be renamed? Is renaming a university so costly as to be unthinkable?"[41]

In the end, the Yale controversy fizzled out amid disagreement among historians over the degree of Elihu Yale's involvement in the slave trade. Nonetheless, the episode shows that other institutions may one day face uncomfortable questions about their own founders, donors, and honorees.

Free Speech in Action

As cancel culture has come to grips with American history, it has uncovered hidden or ignored instances of racism, insensitivity, or exploitation. Progressives have called for a reckoning with figures like Confederate generals who once were honored with statues or monuments. They have rejected books, movies, and songs considered to be offensive, making way for new authors and new works.

Opinions about cancel culture tend to diverge along partisan lines. Many on the left claim that conservatives use cancel culture merely as a scare tactic in the culture wars. Some say that cancel culture really does not exist. But Kevin Drum, a progressive writer for the *Nation*, sees a problem with this viewpoint. "Please don't insult my intelligence by pretending that wokeness and cancel culture are all just figments of the conservative imagination," says Drum. "Sure, they overreact to this stuff, but it really exists, it really is a liberal invention."[42]

When conservatives argue that cancel culture stifles free speech, progressives respond that it does just the opposite— that it is free speech in action, seeking social justice and holding people accountable. But free speech requires the give-and-take of voicing strong opinions without fear. "We need to be open to having conversations with folks we disagree with," says liberal opinion columnist Charles T. Clark, "and we need to simultaneously support holding people accountable for harmful or hateful actions they might engage in. We can't do that honestly, though, unless we hold ourselves accountable as well."[43]

"We need to be open to having conversations with folks we disagree with, and we need to simultaneously support holding people accountable for harmful or hateful actions they might engage in. We can't do that honestly, though, unless we hold ourselves accountable as well."[43]

—Charles T. Clark, opinion columnist

SOURCE NOTES

Introduction: A Controversial Trend

1. Quoted in Michael Levenson, "Georgetown Law Fires Professor for 'Abhorrent' Remarks About Black Students," *New York Times*, March 11, 2021. www.nytimes.com.
2. Quoted in Joseph Wilkinson, "Georgetown Law Professor Trashes Black Students on Zoom Call, Gets Fired," *New York Daily News*, March 11, 2021. www.nydailynews.com.
3. Quoted in Brooke Kato, "What Is Cancel Culture? Everything to Know About the Toxic Online Trend," *New York Post*, June 25, 2021. www.nypost.com.
4. Quoted in *New York Times*, "What Students Are Saying About Cancel Culture, Friendly Celebrity Battles and Finding Escape," November 19, 2020. www.nytimes.com.

Chapter One: What Is Cancel Culture?

5. Quoted in Lisa Respers France, "Kevin Hart on Cancel Culture: 'I Understand People Are Human,'" CNN, June 14, 2021. www.cnn.com.
6. Quoted in Jennifer Graham, "If You Think Cancel Culture Isn't a Problem, You Might Be a Democrat," *Salt Lake City (UT) Deseret News*, February 20, 2021. www.deseret.com.
7. Quoted in Aja Romano, "Why We Can't Stop Fighting About Cancel Culture," Vox, August 25, 2020. www.vox.com.
8. Quoted in Clyde McGrady, "The Strange Journey of 'Cancel,' from a Black-Culture Punchline to a White-Grievance Watchword," *Washington Post*, April 2, 2021. www.washingtonpost.com.
9. Quoted in Sarah Maslin Nir, "White Woman Is Fired After Calling Police on Black Man in Central Park," *New York Times*, May 26, 2020. www.nytimes.com.
10. Quoted in Sarah Ellison and Jeremy Barr, "A Star Reporter's Resignation, a Racial Slur and a Newsroom Divided: Inside the Fallout at the *New York Times*," *Washington Post*, February 12, 2021. www.washingtonpost.com.
11. Douglas Blair, "Cancel Culture Comes for All: How 10-Year-Old Tweets Cost This Journalist Her Job," Daily Signal, March 24, 2021. www.dailysignal.com.

12. Quoted in Lily Hay Newman, "What to Do If You're Being Doxed," *Wired*, December 9, 2017. www.wired.com.
13. Quoted in Romano, "Why We Can't Stop Fighting About Cancel Culture."

Chapter Two: The #MeToo Movement

14. Quoted in Pelin Unker, "#MeToo Movement Arrives in Turkey," DW, December 17, 2020. www.dw.com.
15. Quoted in Unker, "#MeToo Movement Arrives in Turkey."
16. Quoted in Aisha Harris, "She Founded Me Too. Now She Wants to Move Past the Trauma," *New York Times*, October 15, 2018. www.nytimes.com.
17. Quoted in BBC, "Tom Hanks Says No Way Back for Harvey Weinstein," October 19, 2017. www.bbc.com.
18. Quoted in Ryan Lattanzio, "Spike Lee Apologizes for Defending Woody Allen Against Cancel Culture," IndieWire, June 13, 2020. www.indiewire.com.
19. Quoted in Lattanzio, "Spike Lee Apologizes for Defending Woody Allen Against Cancel Culture."
20. Quoted in NPR, "READ: Christine Blasey Ford's Opening Statement for Senate Hearing," September 26, 2018. www.npr.com.
21. Quoted in Jen Kirby, "Read: Brett Kavanaugh's Angry, Emotional Opening Statement," Vox, September 27, 2018. www.vox.com.
22. Maureen Dowd, "Joe Says It Ain't So," *New York Times*, May 2, 2020. www.nytimes.com.

Chapter Three: Cancel Culture and Political Speech

23. Quoted in Jon Skolnik, "Alan Dershowitz Complained About Anti-Trump Tweets," Salon, March 24, 2021. www.salon.com.
24. Quoted in Skolnik, "Alan Dershowitz Complained About Anti-Trump Tweets."
25. Quoted in Jillian Kay Melchior, "A Twitter Mob Takes Down an Administrator at Michigan State," *Wall Street Journal*, June 25, 2020. www.wsj.com.
26. Quoted in Melchior, "A Twitter Mob Takes Down an Administrator at Michigan State."
27. Quoted in Thomas Giery Pudney, "Cornell Issues Statement Denouncing Professor's Tweets," Ithaca Voice, June 5, 2020. https://ithacavoice.com.
28. Quoted in Meghna Maharishi, "Collum Steps Down from Top Chemistry Department Position amid Intense Backlash over Tweets Defending Alleged Police Brutality," *Cornell Daily Sun*, June 8, 2020. www.cornellsun.com.

29. Quoted in Doha Madani and Dylan Byers, "*New York Times* Opinion Editor Resigns amid Fallout over Op-Ed Calling on Military to Quell Protests," NBC News, June 7, 2020. www.nbcnews.com.
30. Quoted in Shannon Bond and Avie Schneider, "Trump Threatens to Shut Down Social Media After Twitter Adds Warning to His Tweets," NPR, May 27, 2020. www.npr.org.
31. Quoted in Mark Moore, "World Leaders Speak Out Against Twitter Suspending Trump's Account," *New York Post*, January 12, 2021. www.nypost.com.
32. Quoted in Emily S. Rueb and Derrick Bryson Taylor, "Obama on Call-Out Culture: 'That's Not Activism,'" *New York Times*, October 31, 2019. www.nytimes.com.

Chapter Four: Reexamining the Past

33. *Daily News* Editorial Board, "Our Songs, Our Eras: The Major League Mistake of Judging Kate Smith by Today's Standards," *New York Daily News*, April 23, 2019. www.nydailynews.com.
34. Quoted in Trevor Hunnicutt, "Biden: Confederate Monuments Belong in Museums, Not Public Squares," Reuters, June 30, 2020. www.reuters.com.
35. Quoted in Politico, "Robert E. Lee Statue Removed in Charlottesville," July 10, 2021. www.politico.com.
36. Quoted in 3CBS Philly, "Trump: 'Are We Gonna Take Down Statues to George Washington?,'" August 15, 2017. https://philadelphia.cbslocal.com.
37. Quoted in Dartunorro Clark, "Statues of Washington, Jefferson Aren't 'Next,' but It's Complicated, Historians Say," NBC News, August 18, 2017. www.nbcnews.com.
38. Sebastian Smee, "Pulling Down Confederate Statues Is a Powerful Statement. But It Won't Erase the Shame," *Washington Post*, June 12, 2020. www.washingtonpost.com.
39. Quoted in Alex Ward, "The Racist History Behind the 10 US Army Facilities Named After Confederate Leaders," Vox, June 9, 2020. www.vox.com.
40. Quoted in Ward, "The Racist History Behind the 10 US Army Facilities Named After Confederate Leaders."
41. Quoted in Valerie Pavilonis, "'Cancel Yale'? Not Likely," *Yale Daily News*, June 28, 2020. www.yaledailynews.com.
42. Kevin Drum, "If You Hate the Culture Wars, Blame Liberals," Jabberwocking, July 3, 2021. www.jabberwocking.com.
43. Charles T. Clark, "Column: A Question We Should Ask Ourselves Before We Back Any Effort to 'Cancel' Someone," *San Diego Union-Tribune*, May 28, 2021. www.sandiegouniontribune.com.

DIFFERING VIEWS:
ACCOUNTABILITY OR PUNISHMENT?

When a person gets called out on social media, is this accountability or punishment? In a Pew Research Center poll on the topic of cancel culture, 58 percent said it is accountability; 38 percent described it as punishment. These are some of the views expressed in the poll.

Why Is It Accountability?

"Calling out offensive content forces people to confront the issue as to whether their content is actually racist, and if it is, to account for their motive in posting it."
—Man, 30s, Conservative Republican

"Because offensive content that is posted allows for the offender to feel more brash with their beliefs while also feeling safe behind the virtual barrier of the internet. However, being called out by someone in the virtual sense can check a person's brazen comments and highlight that their belief is not okay and offensive ... which hopefully causes them to reflect and reevaluate the offensive nature of this content."
—Woman, 20s, Moderate Democrat

"With calling out culture, people look closer at their actions, forcing them to examine what they are doing, why they are doing it, and what are the consequences of said actions."
—Man, 30s, Liberal Democrat

"People need to confront hate when they see hate. People need to confront the dark past [that] is haunting our country. Calling out offensive content is holding people to the standard of what America should be."
—Woman, 30s, Liberal Democrat

"Views expressed online are just as damaging if not more damaging than views expressed in person. People who promote and validate views that hurt other people should have to deal with the consequences of their actions."
—Identifies gender in some other way, 20s, Liberal Democrat

Why Is It Punishment?

"Others are entitled to their opinion, and too often it isn't about having a discussion but berating others for not agreeing with our point of view."
—Woman, 20s, Conservative Republican

"We have freedom of speech in this country. I think you should be able to post whatever you want. It's a free country. If you don't like it, keep scrolling. But people will yell and get upset if they find it offensive and cry like babies."
—Woman, 30s, Conservative Republican

"Social media is designed for people to express their opinions and feelings unique to the individual. A lot of times, people jump down the throats of anything that doesn't align with their views. So nowadays, cancel culture is a thing and too many people want to cancel anyone with an opinion that is considered not politically correct ... You can't try and silence everyone who has an opposing viewpoint to yours."
—Man, 30s, Liberal Democrat

"Many times, we cannot see the source or reasoning or driving forces from what we see online. Although calling out offensive content holds many people and organizations to a higher standard and is necessary and vital, often social media can have an effect of a mob mentality and swift judgement when situations are more complex."
—Woman, 20s, Liberal Democrat

"When people post online, it should be a free platform of expression and others should not be calling people out for their own opinions, just because they differ from their own. Social media can be punishing because when others target someone for their thoughts it can be hurtful or degrading. If someone doesn't like another person's opinion they should unfollow or keep scrolling—not 'call each other out.'"
—Woman, 20s, Conservative Republican

Source: Emily A. Vogels et al., "Americans and 'Cancel Culture': Where Some See Calls for Accountability, Others See Censorship, Punishment," Pew Research Center, May 19, 2021. www.pewresearch.org.

Books

Alan Dershowitz, *Cancel Culture: The Latest Attack on Free Speech and Due Process*. New York: Hot Books, 2020.

Carly Gieseler, *The Voices of #MeToo: From Grassroots Activism to a Viral Roar*. Washington, DC: Rowman & Littlefield, 2019.

James Gill and Howard Hunter, *Tearing Down the Lost Cause: The Removal of New Orleans's Confederate Statues*. Jackson: University Press of Mississippi, 2021.

Dan Kovalik, *Cancel This Book: The Progressive Case Against Cancel Culture*. New York: Hot Books, 2021.

Rachel B. Vogelstein and Meighan Stone, *Awakening: #MeToo and the Global Fight for Women's Rights*. New York: Public Affairs, 2021.

Internet Sources

Dani Di Placido, "The Harper's Letter, Bari Weiss and Tucker Carlson," *Forbes*, July 14, 2020. www.forbes.com.

Sarah Hagi, "Cancel Culture Is Not Real—at Least Not in the Way People Think," *Time*, November 21, 2019. https://time.com.

Aisha Harris, "She Founded Me Too. Now She Wants to Move Past the Trauma," *New York Times*, October 15, 2018. www.nytimes.com.

Mary Harris, "How Democrats Can Win the Fight over Cancel Culture," Slate, April 14, 2021. https://slate.com.

Aja Romano, "The Second Wave of 'Cancel Culture,'" Vox, May 5, 2021. www.vox.com.

Sanam Yar and Jonah Engel Bromwich, "Tales from the Teenage Cancel Culture," *New York Times*, October 31, 2019. www.nytimes.com.

Websites

Freedom Forum

www.freedomforum.org

The Freedom Forum describes its mission as fostering First Amendment freedoms for all. It seeks to raise awareness about these freedoms through education, advocacy, and action, sharing the stories of Americans who exercise their right to ignite change. One recent post on the website was titled "Cancel Culture Can Chill Free Speech; It's Also Free Speech in Action."

Heritage Foundation

www.heritage.org

The Heritage Foundation performs research and pursues solutions to support freedom, opportunity, and prosperity in America. The foundation's website features articles about the free-speech aspects of the cancel culture phenomenon.

me too.

https://metoomvmt.org

The #MeToo movement focuses on assisting survivors of sexual harassment and assault, including young people, queer, trans, the disabled, Black women and girls, and all communities of color. The website features information about organizing against sexual violence, survivor leadership training, and online courses for creating safe campuses.

Reason.com

https://reason.com

This website for the print magazine compiles all the publication's articles on cancel culture and related topics. Among the features are an interview with Abigail Shrier titled "Trans Activists, Cancel Culture, and the Future of Free Expression," and "Melissa Chen on Fighting Wokeness at Home and Radicalism Abroad."

INDEX

Note: Boldface page numbers indicate illustrations.

Aaron, Hank, 35
Ahmad, Hassan, 4
Ailes, Roger, 22
Allen, Woody, 6, 26–27
Alphan, Melis, 21
American Black culture
  use of "cancel" in
    as example of Black humor and
      pride, 12
    as form of power, 10, 13
    history of, 10, 19
    "woke" and, 13
art and political correctness, 18
Ataselim, Fidan, 21
Atlantic (magazine), 36

Baquet, Dean, 15
Barr, Roseanne, 5
#BelieveWomen, 27–29
Bennet, James, 37, 38
Berlin, Irving, 43
Biden, Joe, 30–31, 45, 50, 52
Biles, Simone, 26
Blair, Douglas, 17
Boston, 48–49
Bottoms, Keisha Lance, 35
Brown, Anthony, 50–51
Bryant, Zyahna, 46
Buck, Ken, 39
Burke, Tarana, 21, **22**, 23

Calhoun, John C., 52
call-out culture, 5–6
cancel culture
  alternative term for, 5–6
  described, 5, 9
  history of term, 10, 19
  public's definitions of, **11**
#CancelYale campaign, 53
Cardona, Miguel, 30
Cato Institute, 36
Cernovich, Mike, 17

Cesario, Joe, 34
Charlottesville, Virginia, **46**, 46–47
Cheney, Liz, 39
Chow, Keith, 18
Clark, Charles T., 54
Colak, Ibrahim, 20
Collum, David, 34–35
Communications Decency Act (1996),
  52
Confederate monuments, 45–47, **46**
Confederate symbols, 45–47, **46**,
  50–52, **51**
consequences of cancel culture
  empowerment of individuals, 10,
    13, 19
  imprisonment, 26
  increase in reporting sex crimes,
    30
  loss of employment, 30
    Bennet, 37–38
    Amy Cooper, 14–15
    at Fox News, 22
    in Hollywood, 27
    Kaepernick, 14
    Bandy Lee, 33
    McCammond, 16–17
    McNeil, 15
    Sellers, 4–5
    at Uber, 22
    Wynn, 25
  political figures and, 28–31, 39
Cooper, Amy, 14–15
Cooper, Barry Michael, 12–13
Cooper, Christian, 14–15
Cotton, Joe, 37–38

Dershowitz, Alan, 32, **33**
DeVos, Betsy, 30
Douglas, Gabby, 26
Dowd, Maureen, 31
doxing, 17–18
Drum, Kevin, 53–54

entertainment industry. *See* Hollywood/
  entertainment industry

Facebook, 40
Fallon, Jimmy, 15–16
Farrow, Dylan, 26
Federal Bureau of Investigation (FBI), 26
Floyd, George, protests, **16**, **37**
    Cotton op-ed in *New York Times*, 37–38
    Gone with the Wind removal and disclaimers
        by HBO Max, 48
    racist tweets and, 15
    removal of statues, 45
Ford, Christine Blasey, 28–29, **29**, 31
forgiveness, 7, 17
Fowler, Susan, 21–22
Fox News, 22
free speech
    cancel culture and, 9, 37
    fear and, 54
    "woke" political outlook and, 7

Galperin, Eva, 18
Gavin, Wilson, 41
Glickman, Lawrence, 10
"God Bless America" (Berlin), 43
Gone with the Wind (movie), 48
Grueskin, Bill, 15
Gunn, James, 17

Halperin, Mark, 24
Harper's Magazine, 7
Hart, Kevin, 8–9
history
    disclaimers on films, 48–49
    reexamination of, 45
    removal or vandalism of statues, 45–49, **46**
Hollywood/entertainment industry
    casting of movies, 18
    disclaimers on films and, 48–49
    sexual harassment in, 23–24, 26–27
homophobia, accusations of, 17
Hopper, Grace Murray, 52
Hsu, Stephen, 34
Hudley, Anne Charity, 19
Huffington Post, 9

Indianapolis Star (newspaper), 26

Jackson, Peter, 23
Jackson, Thomas "Stonewall," 46
Jacoby, Jeff, 36
Johansson, Scarlett, 18
Jolie, Angelina, 23
Judd, Ashley, 23

Kaepernick, Colin, 14
Kalanick, Travis, 22
"Karens," 14
Kavanaugh, Brett, 28–29

Krystal, John, 32–33

Lauer, Matt, 24
Lee, Bandy, 32–33
Lee, Robert E., 45–46, **46**
Lee, Spike, 27
"A Letter on Justice and Open Debate"
    (Harper's Magazine), 7
Levine, James, 24
López Obrador, Andrés Manuel, 40
Louis C.K., 24

Major League Baseball (MLB) All-Star Game
    (2021), 35
Maroney, McKayla, 26
#MayYouLoseSleep, 20–21
McCammond, Alexi, 16–17
McCorkel, Jill, 6–7
McCormack, Michael, 40
McDaniel, Hattie, 48
McGowan, Rose, 23
McNeil, Donald, Jr., 15
Merkel, Angela, 40
#MeToo movement, 6, 21
movies, casting, 18

NASCAR, 50, **51**
Nassar, Larry, 26
National Defense Authorization Act (2021), 50
New Orleans, 47–48
New York City Central Park incident, 14–15
New York Daily News (newspaper), 44
New Yorker (magazine), 23
New York Times (newspaper), 7, 15, 22–23, 30,
    31, 37–38
Norris, Pippa, 36
Northam, Ralph, 16

Obama, Barack, 30, 42
O'Reilly, Bill, 6, 22
Oreskes, Michael, 24

Paltrow, Gwyneth, 23
Pelosi, Nancy, 31
Phillips, Nathan, 41
political speech
    attitude toward, 9
    Cheney, 39
    Cornell University, 34–35
    divisions reinforced by, 6–7
    history of cancel culture in, 10
    Michigan State University (MSU), 34
    New York Times and, 37–38
    personal attacks and, 41–42
    Section 230 and, 52
    universities and
        loss of employment, 4–5, 33

renamings of areas, 52–53
    self-censorship, 36–37
Pollack, Martha E., 35
public opinion, 7, 9
    changing names of military bases named for
        Confederate commanders, 51–52
    meaning of phrase "cancel culture," **11**
    sexual harassment claims, 27–28
    stating political beliefs, 37

racism, accusations of
    Collum, 34–35
    Amy Cooper, 14–15
    Fallon, 15–16
    Georgia legislature, 35
    Gone with the Wind, 48
    Hsu, 34
    Johansson, 18
    Kaepernick, 14
    McCammond, 16–17
    McNeil, 15
    Northam, 16
    Sellers, 4–5
    Smith, 43–44
    Wilson, 52
Raisman, Aly, 26
Reade, Tara, 30–31
Reid, Eric, 14
Richmond, Virginia, 48
Ridley, John, 48
Robinson, Nathan, 53
Rodgers, Nile, 10
Rose, Charlie, 24

Salinger, Leyla, 20
Sandmann, Nicholas, 41–42
Section 230, 52
self-censorship, 36–37
Sellers, Sandra, 4–5
sexual harassment
    accusations of
        believing women's, 27–28
        Biden, 30–31
        at Fox News, 22
        in Hollywood/entertainment industry,
            23–24, 26–27
        Kavanaugh, 28–29
        at Uber, 22
        USA Gymnastics women's team, 26
        US Department of Education rulings, 30
        by Wynn, 25
    increase in reporting of, 30
"she said–he said" dilemma, 28
slave owners, statues of, 47–48
Smee, Sebastian, 49
Smith, Kate, 43–44, **44**
social media

doxing on, 17–18
as empowering those without power, 6
immediacy of reactions on, 11–12
legal liability of, 52
materials in archives, 16–17
private comments posted on, 4
rise of cancel culture and, 5, **6**, 11
    See also Twitter
Sorvino, Mira, 23
Spacey, Kevin, 6, 24
statues, removal or vandalism of, 45–50, **46**
Suber, Malcolm, 47–48

Take 'Em Down NOLA, 47–48
teenagers, attitude toward cancel culture, 7
Teen Vogue (magazine), 16–17
Toptas, Hasan Ali, 20
Treanor, William, 4–5
Trump, Donald, **33**
    attack on cancel culture, 9
    Facebook and, 40
    removal or vandalism of statues and, 47, 50
    Twitter and, 38–40, **40**
    US Department of Education sexual
        harassment ruling under, 30
    West and, 10, **12**
Turkey, 20–21
Twitter
    #CancelYale campaign, 53
    Hart and, 8
    immediacy of reactions on, 11–12
    #MeToo movement, 6, 21
    policy on tweets deemed to be false, 38
    Sellers and, 4–5
    sharing of sexual harassment episodes on, 23
    Trump and, 38–40, **40**
    in Turkey, 20–21

Uber, 21–22
Unite the Right rally, 46–47
USA Gymnastics, 26
US Army bases, 50–52
US Department of Education, 30

Wall Street Journal (newspaper), 25
Washington Post (newspaper), 49
Weinstein, Harvey, 6, 23, 24, **25**
Wellman, Fred, 51
West, Kanye, 10, **12**
Wilson, Woodrow, 52
"woke"
    genesis of, 13
    political outlook and, 5, 7, 14
Wynn, Steve, 25

Yale, Elihu, 53
YouGov, 9

PICTURE CREDITS